To:

From:

Go for It, Girlfriend!

Written and photographed by

Kelly Povo

PETER PAUPER PRESS, INC.
WHITE PLAINS, NEW YORK

Designed by Heather Zschock

Copyright © 2004 Kelly Povo
www.kellypovo.com

Published by Peter Pauper Press, Inc.
202 Mamaroneck Avenue
White Plains, NY 10601
All rights reserved
ISBN 978-0-88088-364-1
Printed in China
7 6 5 4

Visit us at www.peterpauper.om

Go for It, Girlfriend!

Hey, Friend!

Sometimes your trip down life's highway gets BUMPY.

Some days even clean underwear doesn't perk you up. When you forget just how great you really are, DON'T WORRY. I remember. For those days when you lose your way, here are some "travel tips" to help YOU remember:

You, dear friend, are the best.

You're a star.

I believe in you...

Believe in yourself.

Travel your own road.

Pack light, all you need is yourself.
Stay off the beaten path.

Life's an adventure.

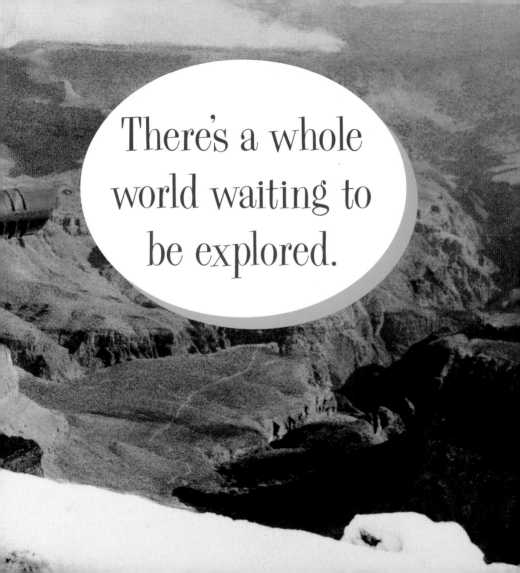

There's a whole world waiting to be explored.

Where there's a will, there's a way!

It's never too late to get started.

Make your own music.

Try something new every day.

Speak softly and carry a big wrench.

One crisis at a time.
You can handle anything.

Take time to putter around.

Get teed up, not teed off.

Take your best swing.

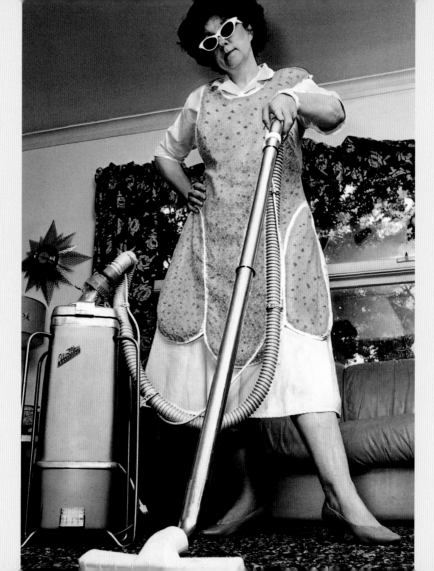

Learn when to say

"NO,"

and when to say

"YES."

If you can't
get under it,
get over it.

Lower your expectations.

Life has its ups and downs.

If you're down,
you'll be up
again soon.

Hang on tight!

If you believe in
yourself, you'll
never be defeated.

Ride the waves—
just bring a friend.

Don't be afraid to get your feet wet.

Take the plunge!

Be open to something new. Dive right in.

Do something monumental.

You're a work
of art.

✦

Take your time,
don't Rushmore.

Make your mark in the world.

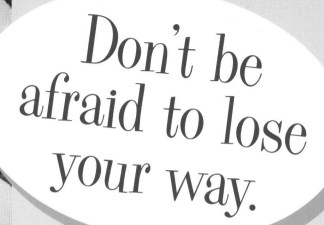

Don't be afraid to lose your way.

Share the road.

✦

If you're lost, you're not
alone. Remember,
you can ask for help.

Yes, you can-can.

✦

One step at a time.
When all else
fails, dance.

Dream a little.

Laugh
a lot.

Hang on to your friends.

✦

Things are not always as they appear.

✦

Remember, there are two sides to every story. Don't compare yourself to others.

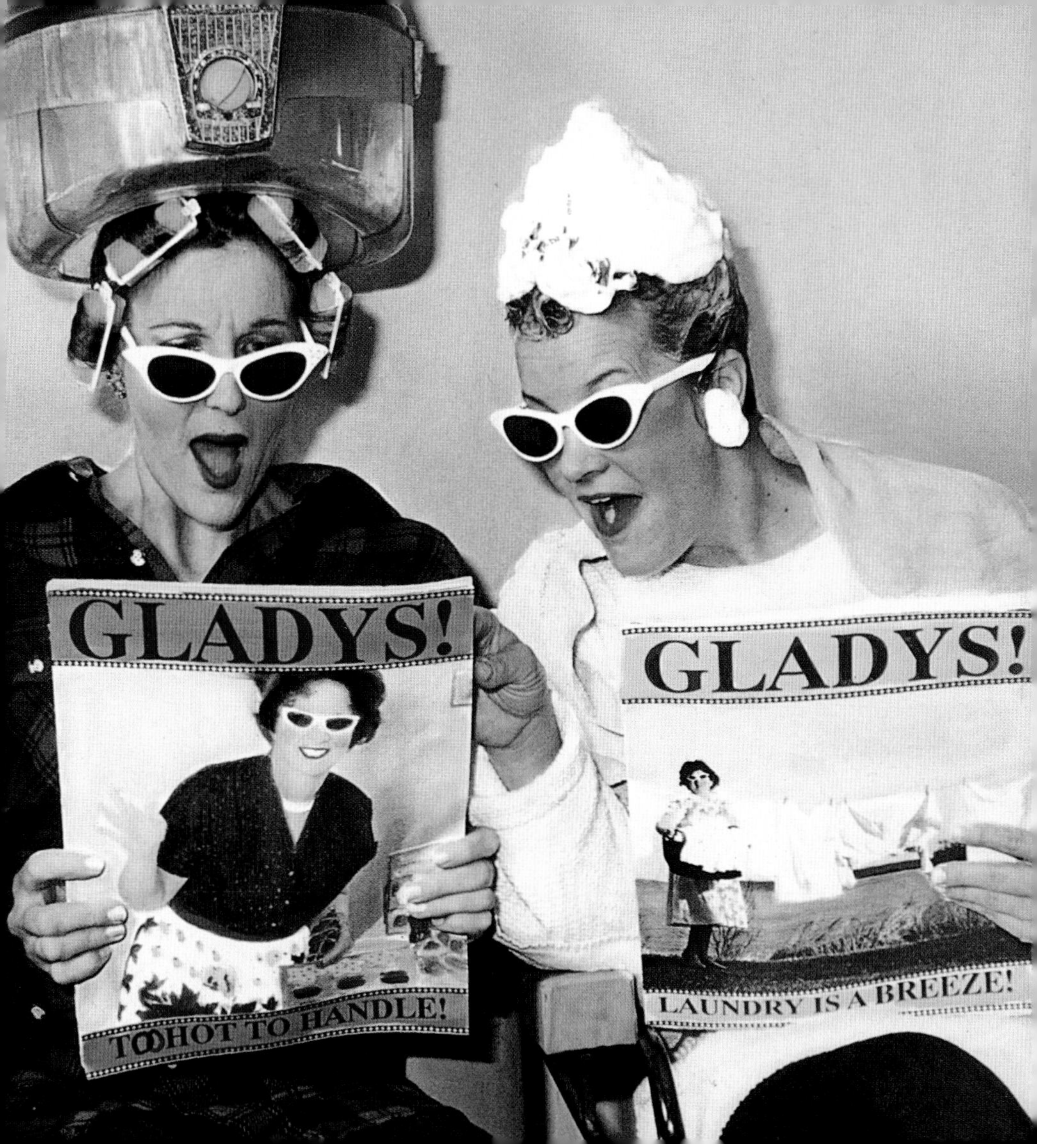
GLADYS!
TOO HOT TO HANDLE!
GLADYS!
LAUNDRY IS A BREEZE!

Do things
your own
way.

Use your head.

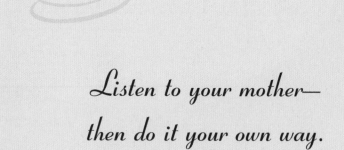

Listen to your mother—
then do it your own way.

✦

Sometimes it's good to shake things up.

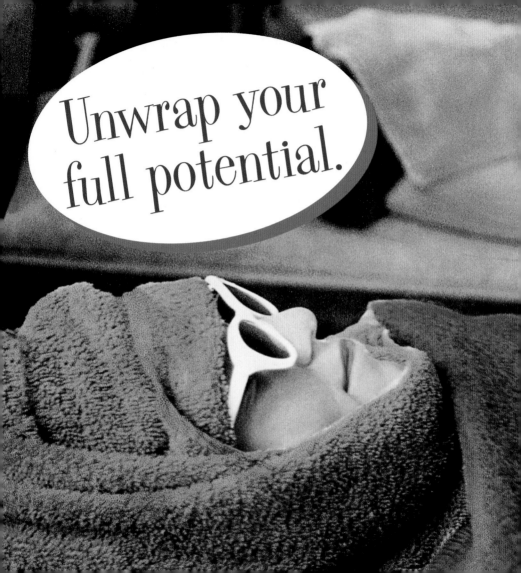

Don't hide behind your fears.

✦

Don't throw in the towel—

get a wrap instead.

Don't sweat it—you're still in the game!

*Things always have a way of
ironing themselves out.*

✦

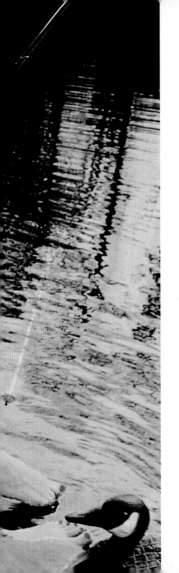

Go with the flow.

✦

You may feel like you're up

a creek, but remember,

you still have a paddle.

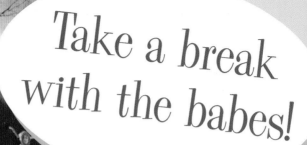

Take a break with the babes!

*The best things
in life come in
small packages.*

Surround yourself with your favorite things.

It's true, you never know what is going to pop up in your life ...

Unplug everything and just relax.

Let others pamper you— you're worth it!

◆

Learn to receive.

Remember, sharing makes life sweeter!

✦

Spend some time in the great outdoors.

You don't always have to act like a lady.

Leave your worries behind you.

✦

Got a sad tale? I hear you.

Talk it out with your friends.

You belong.

◆

Smile!

The grass is green

wherever you are!

In the
game of life,
you will
always be
a winner.

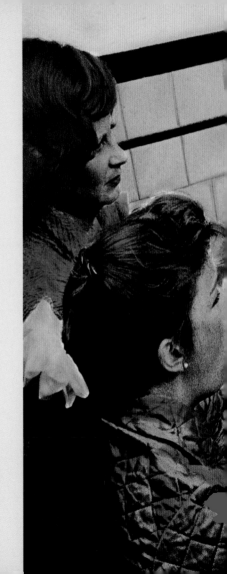

You're perfect just the way you are.

✦

You're a star.

You'll be back in the saddle again soon.

✦

Happy trails to you.